Bringing Back the Fire

Kimberly L. Becker

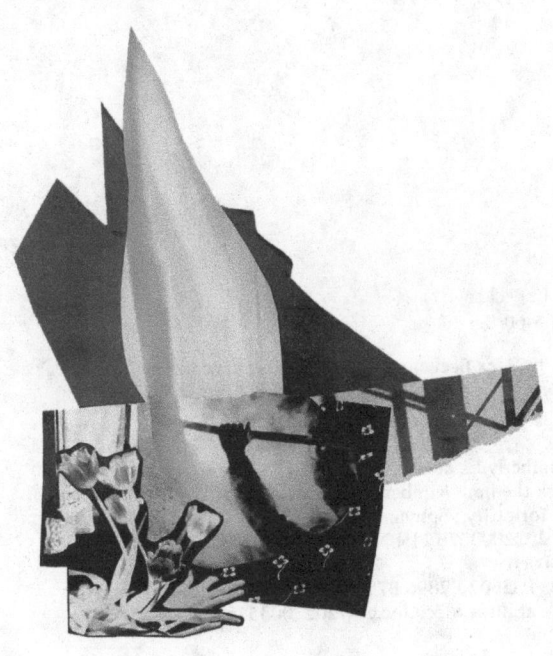

Spuyten Duyvil
New York City

Cover art, "Stoke" by Alex Becker www.artbyalexbecker.com

Library of Congress Cataloging-in-Publication Data

Names: Becker, Kimberly L., author.
Title: Bringing back the fire / Kimberly L. Becker.
Description: New York City : Spuyten Duyvil, [2022] |
Identifiers: LCCN 2022003576 | ISBN 9781956005608 (paperback)
Subjects: LCGFT: Poetry.
Classification: LCC PS3602.E2896 B75 2022 | DDC 811/.6--dc23
LC record available at https://lccn.loc.gov/2022003576

For Alex, as ever

DARKNESS

LIGHT

Darkness

I see the milestones dwindling/toward the horizon/and the slow fires trailing/from the abandoned camp-sites,/over which scavenger angels/wheel on heavy wings.

   —Stanley Kunitz, from "The Layers"

Even death who is the chief of everything on this earth (all undertakings, all matters of human form) will wash his hands, stop to rest under the cottonwood before taking you from me on the back of his horse.

   —Joy Harjo, from "Songs from the House of Death, or How to Make it Through to the End of a Relationship"

AFFIXING THE HALO
(medical instrument placed
prior to stereotactic brain surgery)

It's hard to get a halo (harder than you think)
First off, the anxiety of wondering will it hurt?
Yes, it will
So the nurse starts an IV of calming medication
in your receiving vein
and soon you don't mind
as much when the neurosurgeon in white
arrives like a stern god and places the heavy halo
on your head and marks the points of contact
He then injects multiple numbing shots that feel
like bad bee stings
(to numb, you have to hurt)
where they're going to attach this
heavy nimbus
which they do,
with bolts
like Frankenstein's monster
(everyone says *Frankenstein,*
but he was the creator, remember?
and a woman wrote the book,
so she should know how men create
to replicate their own misshapen form)
The halo is heavy as hell
(that well-worn simile)
It becomes hard to hold
your head up
with the weight
of this unwieldy glory
And then: the thing is on
You officially have a halo

(but it's not even gold or pretty—
dull metal of a lesser angel)
You dopily take a selfie and send it
to an angel in your life, who immediately texts back,
"that's your next book!" and here we are, folks
and you wonder if heaven, that comforting construct,
is like this—
hard-won halos for fallen angels
and *angel* in Greek means *messenger*,
so what's the message here?
Buck up; hold your head high?
But the halo is heavy; you can barely walk
No way you could fly
even if they managed to screw on wings,
which they don't (the drugs are kicking in)
and anyway,
pain is part of everything
Did you think you'd be exempt?
You don't look angelic or beautiful
you look, frankly, frankensteiningly, ridiculous
You can't blend in when you have a ******* halo on your head
(you redact your curse the opposite of how G*d is redacted out of piety)
People part as you pass unsteadily
They might have fancied they wanted a halo of their own,
but now they're not so sure
Not when they see the blood where the halo is anchored
Some blood sacrifice always seem to be required,
so you try to be a good sport about it
and offer willingly
(your father always called you *sport*;
what was up with that? He's dead
and maybe knows more about angels
than you ever will)
Oh, and get this: they will use the halo to bolt you to the table

for radiation!
You will become radiant
before severe queasiness will follow
Uneasy is the head that wears a halo

APPARATUS

The derricks nodding their heads
over the Bakken with its layers
extracting need on need
These machines not unlike the halo on your head,
serving a purpose
The quiet land covered in patterned color not unlike a quilt
Where to start?
In medias res?
No, the best place to start is where you are
It's a matter of scale
variations on need
distortions of the same
muted colors from drought versus the verdant green of home
leaving home to find home after all

THEY SAID YOU WON'T REMEMBER

as heavy black mask came down with ether
as Versed coursed through your veins
as Propofol bloomed in your blood,
but a part of you did and does
Where does the mind go
when the body undergoes
and undergoes?
The D & C after miscarriage
in an Alabama
emergency room
and later, bright green bile
and fever,
your surgeon asking
how could he do that?
upon finding out your husband
had left you there
Same surgeon
offering to send a private
jet to fly you from Princeton to Boston
You *do* remember, but it is like looking through
crackled glass
like ice crackling on branches
The pretty dot of acid
someone offered you in Germany:
you didn't take it
Your mind went away enough
on its own
Binge-watching dreams:
there's the bear again
there the man in bandages like a mummy
there the disemboweled animals
there the blood the knife the gun the razor blades

only sometimes a peaceful intermission
where ancestors danced
on the bald of the mountain,
inviting you in to the circle
Vivid lucidity of blood memory
Break from suffering
or acceptance that makes it bearable
Rise of smoke from cedar and tobacco
Slow and painful process of healing from within
Re-membering of what was dismembered
Re-grafting of skin and bone and mind and spirit
to what is whole and hopes to hold in this fragile fractured life

VENTUS

This wind whittles down to essential form
Riderless horses returned from Little Big Horn

Always we are pulled towards the idea of home
Water and wind form cannonballs of stone

We trade words of greeting: NAheesa atistit/osd sunalei
Wind loosens our hair, growing out after grief

Shame burns like flares on the Bakken
Wind tosses flames like horses' manes

In Germany, sirocco from Spain a soft caress
Distances deceive in this vast space

Palms almost touching, energy palpable
To track Aurora, I download an app,

imagine us lying magnetized under neon skies
You say the Missouri is called the Great Mystery

I introduce myself as I would to any person
You point out strong current's direction

under what I perceived as only swirling surface
We remember flooding of ancestral

homelands, dams built to harness force
while river and wind keep adjusting course

Doppelgängerin

The gun is pointed at you, armed appendage
This won't end well
It never does
She in an incongruous purple suit
Instead of running away,
you dive at her legs
knocking her off balance
She goes down
the gun goes off
glass shatters
there are screams,
one of which you recognize as yours
She is you
You have always fought against yourself
seeking balance
You must disarm yourself
It was you all along
In this way you become unafraid
You become instead someone to be feared

FLOW

Blood fills vial dark as oil
Human body/body of the land,
each with its history of treachery

With each heartbeat,
rush of blood in ear, ocean within,
I hear thunder of bison, of horses,
hoofbeats crossing through time

I see you as a boy riding bareback and falling,
fracturing collarbone then getting back on
Hard to heal when what is broken is never set

Frack forcibly enough and you're bound to find
something releasable in flare
Meanwhile, the waterfalls of home
veil on without me there

Bruise in crook of arm from needle's plunge,
blood under skin seeking reabsorption
into flow of veins

At day's end, I lie awake and count,
not sheep, but all the rivers that I've crossed,
starting backwards
with Missouri

NEST

for Helen and John

Your great aunt lay on the couch
out of reach
brain nested in tumor
Your mother approached
and held her hand and spoke words
you couldn't hear
To your shame, you failed to do the same

Years later you sit with your patient
brain also tumored
making small amend
for earlier omission
to be a ministry of presence
now knowing that the dying are closer to life
than even the living

At the beach we turn away
from the crushed baby bird
amid perfect half of pale teal speckled eggshell
We shield our eyes from that naked twisted
beak and body,
but the eggshell we salvage as object for still life
Fallen nest is never found

SURRENDER

for Malaika

Salt of submission
along with other chemicals
Falling, you notice branches
you might grasp, but don't
Falling, you look up into unbiased blue
Falling, you pass a solitary eagle
and take that as a sign of blessing
It's not so bad,
not like the terror underwater
under crushing
green of wave
and grind of sand
At least no cutting coral here
You keep waiting to hit bottom
It's coming at you fast,
but fear releases into
parachute of hope
you didn't know you had,
jerking you upwards
in mute astonishment
at life

PLUNGE

There are moments when we touch the bottom of the pool
and looking up through prismed blue
are so enchanted that we forget we are among the drowned

SQUARE OF BLUE

Think of any moment of joy
What was its basis? Was it all fantasy
concocted by confused wills,
projections overlapping?

The mountains do not question
their existence
They were formed from friction
like all beauty

Hierarchy of needs is a fallacy
We need everything at once
So many ways to fail to
thrive

Mount the stairs to the hayloft
Look out onto blue sky square—
hanging place,
shooting place

Knocking from within barn walls
Spirits saying,
we, too, lived with unmet needs
we, too, need attention

Let go of attachments
Strive for acceptance;
otherwise it won't get easier,
even on the other side

CALL

You called when I was in Atlanta,
but I couldn't answer

I was at a conference and busy, yes,
but also to have heard your voice

would have taken strength I needed
to drive long hours back North

so instead I stop at our sacred places,
impromptu pilgrimage

to Etowah Mounds—
climbing highest mound to pray—

then on to New Echota
proud capitol where The Trail of Tears started

These are the calls we have to answer,
the ones from home to heart,

the ones that go deeper
even than words

Skipping tourist shop,
I reach for one red leaf

from this place of strength and grief,
offering thanks.

My tears are for self,
but also from deeper source

As I merge back on the highway
it starts to rain and I greet it

with a word you taught me
that I did not know I remembered,

but that re-members me:
agaska

BADLANDS

for Stephanie

with no coming together there can be no transformation
—Lucretius, *De Rerum Natura*

Bluffs rise above lake where bones are found,
evidence of a spoken life

Someone said he hoped I'd hate it here
I don't

You say you'll show me places that aren't on any map

I disappear into crevices of rock in the badlands
I blend in to the neutral tones of buff and sandstone
I disperse into wind like the paints I saw bolting up the hill
I try to stay grounded, but one time I flew away
when I was in your car and you, knowing how to handle horses,
kept your hand on my leg while I watched from above
and from there could see bison we failed to find on foot
They were ranging on the other side like that time on Shackleford Island
when wild horses eluded me until I saw them huddled on the other
side just as our boat pulled away from shore

My friend says it isn't good to have just one horse, that they need a herd
When my dog died, my friend let me lean against
her horse (holy dog) that in turn allowed me to saddle her with my grief

You say if it's meant to be, it will be
I still spook easily, but less often

The badlands of our lives have lessons to teach
And their own beauty

Media Vita

You tell me you cried when you shot
your first deer and I think of my first-caught trout
all silver and rainbow
eyes fixed, mouth gaping and gasping
So much death for hunger

When I drove back from your place at 3am
all was fog, all unrecognizable in an already strange place
that could have been no place, any place, Germany or
that road from Boone where fog was also so disorienting

I edged forward through landscape erased to soft edges,
silver contour like gelatin print,
knowing there were lakes on either side
where a car could disappear at night in fog
and driver would drown before being discovered
You warn me to watch for moose,
but headlights barely pierce enough to see anything at all

We compare scars
some from dogs, some from ceremony
I will try not to destroy the good
I will become whatever is asked,
anticipate need, shapeshift to what is required,
but you accept me as I am
This is new and frightening

Hoping to find someone's obituary
I find his friend's, also a liar
I keep waiting for the deaths of my enemies
In this way, a part of me is always dying to life
as I remember:

long eyelashes of dead infant in the trauma bay
greenish pallor of dead teenager on Christmas morning,
corpse of a swaddled baby I carried to the morgue

The weight of these images can keep me from seeing
that in the midst of death I am still in life

How to Make it Through to the End of a Conjure

1) Remember the strength of your own medicine

2) Give to others, such as the time
in the hospital on Thanksgiving
when you get a page to visit a man
admitted for attempted suicide
After my wife left and my grandbaby got murdered
I had nothing left, so I laid down in the road
and waited for death

3) Remember your own suffering can enlarge your heart for more
compassion
Remember you are no different in being forgotten
even with your official badge of belonging
You bring your patient a quilt sewn by volunteers
He lays its colors across his lap, smiling through tears,
You order him a holiday meal from the cafeteria
Finally, he is comforted

4) Give away what you most need

OBSIDIAN

It's cold as shit on concrete hospital steps
when you lay a hand on her knee with, *I
don't know what to say except my heart breaks
for you* Her fiancé is brain dead. Irish
lover of fireballs and this woman in pink-
pilled sweater, awash in cigarette smoke and snot
They were supposed to get married in June
Her face is worn and lined with tragedy
Gathering her strength, she howls in protest,
God, if you are real, then fuck you for this!
The wind joins in with chilling draft
People walk past with barely a glance
Death is not news except to the lover
Later you read how heat from Vesuvius
turned a man's brain to obsidian frag-
ments embedded within his skull at death
The mind can only take so much

Q & A

The moon a soft question in morning sky

The dead come back to check on us
and try to tell us when we're moving
                    in the wrong direction

Often we don't listen

The moon a firm answer in night sky

CODES

Two codes run simultaneously in different ED rooms
One survives, but not the one we expect
She's old and beaten up by life
But the businessman, naked save for black dress socks,
is unresponsive and has been down over an hour, even though
the nurse compressing his chest continues her assault
as his flaccid penis with unseeing eye lies exposed and flopping
against his purple scrotum

There is no dignity in death

Finally they call it and we observe a moment of silence
His left arm has fallen free of the gurney and his wedding ring gleams dull
under sterile lights
Only then do we cover his nakedness with clean white sheet
and tell him how sorry we are that we couldn't bring him back
Soon I will hold his phone away from my ear as his widow screams
from another state away

The randomness is what will eat at us after we've gone home
to dogs and kids and those who wear our rings
We hug them tight until they squirm away, laughing
We lie awake listening as they sleep,
invincible in ignorance

TRAUMA BOX

From the dawn parking garage
steam rises like an apparition
or the spirits of those
who died in transit
or in hospital beds
or in the trauma room
while the choreography
of hope tried to outpace death

We each take our places,
while God, pacing the hall
like an expectant father,
is banned from the room
for fainting at the sight of blood
and excrement of delivery

Or maybe he went out for a smoke
while the EMS guy wipes
the backboard of red
while flirting with a nurse
So little lies between
blessing and curse

The room, now emptied,
is strewn with reddened
clothes that detectives
take pictures of,
still lives of lives stilled
We, the actors, who marked
our places, disperse
The lock-down is over

From the dawn parking garage
there is a view of steam
rising like apparitions,
like the spirits of those released,
like our breath in the chill air of death

RED CLAY

In a dream you say goodbye
to a dark-haired woman
and walk away with your old dog,
now gone to spirit
Red clay dirt conceals your feet and paws,
but you are finally grounded

Heimweh

I am far from
mound and mountain
       On these Northern Plains
the wind never ceases,
susurration like the ocean
Astonishment at pelicans
white, not the brown ones last seen
       over Atlantic waves
Dissonance of familiarity
in strange place
       Light insinuates late, aubades early
Wait til winter, you warn me
I learn new language
for this landscape: coulee and kettles
badlands buttes and bluffs
       An eagle dives for prey
grander than ever imagined
Bison trundle over earth
A lone horse stands backlit on a rise
My mouth tries to form the word
for *horse* in your language: *xaawaarúxti'*
       but I still face East to sing
my morning song in Cherokee
       On dusty road framed by primrose
I find three yellow stones
tiny jewels of sun I pass on to my son
before his flight Northeast
       Pelican in pond extends enormous wings
as if to put on coat or cast off cape,
or rather, as if measuring span
between its existence   and my insistence
       on not entirely imagined kinship

both of us between homes
and on the way

                to somewhere else

Spyglass

Fissures in the fontanel
suggest questions to be asked
On the gallows of truth, a single figure against the sky,
the sun a disk of torment in your eyes that also serves to purify

THE FAR LAKE

for Sy

If the lake is too far then take your time arriving
It will still be there
though children clamor
in the backseat
and clouds scroll and unscroll divination

If the lake is too far
then you could set up encampment
and rest along the way
and attend to other needs

If the lake is far,
arriving at the self is further still
When you arrive at the lakeshore, wait for me
I won't be far behind

The lake is far
It's hard to find
It is close by
Closer than you think

Is the lake far?
Yes, it is past the point of almost giving up
It was formed from the crater of anger
It is the shape of a wound that has not closed
No
It is the shape of an uneven circle
It is important to know how it was formed: manmade or real?

Once you are there at the lake
you can swim with the dead from drowned towns flooded for progress
They mirror you, matching you stroke for stroke
they reach and touch your hair, sending you sputtering to the surface
or you can stay on the shore, watchfully watching your children play

When the lake is far
you have to want to reach it
It is not enough to imagine wanting to be there
The momentous events of our lives can go unnoticed by those with
whom we are most intimate

If the lake is too far
try another lake
though you'll always miss the missed one

If the lake is far
ask yourself if you really want to go there
If you do, then yes, go
but if something in you hesitates
and clenches at the thought of loss it will entail,
don't go

The lake is far
I will miss you when you get there

Elemental

Clouds are striated, thinned by keening wind over northern plains
Your shaming cannot reach me here
Cliffs overlooking the lake formed by flood from damning dam
where returned and scalped man hid
This uncontrollable western wind strips bare our needs
Back East, green-gold bird hovers in front of me, humming of hope
Weight of apron against radiation for scan of boy hit by school bus
He keeps apologizing, unaware of avulsion, scalp torn back to reveal skull
       beneath the skin
Buffalo skulls piled then pulled in sacrifice
Water is water the delivery man says, refilling bottle with chemicals
Back home, spring water flows timelessly through spring house
      from generations back

Rounds

It was there before we knew it,
silently rounding, killing few
then starting to take even more
patients/patience; we could not ignore
that this illness was something new

At first we thought it was the flu
Too many dead in ICU
Units spilled onto other floors
while bodies piled up in the morgue
It was there before we even knew

How to tell what is false or true
when what is seen was never viewed?
No return to what was before
We chart with increasing anger
at what we can't cure—we push through
It was there before we knew

Light

I came to explore the wreck./The words are purposes./The words are maps./I came to see the damage that was done/and the treasures that prevail.
  —Adrienne Rich, from "Diving into the Wreck"

...this illusion of some safety to be found/the heavy-footed hoped to silence us/For all of us/this instant and this triumph/We were never meant to survive.../ and when we speak we are afraid/our words will not be heard/nor welcomed/but when we are silent/we are still afraid/So it is better to speak/ remembering/ we were never meant to survive.
  —Audre Lorde, from "A Litany for Survival"

Light

EMBER

Now you make a new language from ember of the old
Former words bound you to what you knew,
to what you thought you deserved
Now you are ready for your new name
written in sparks that fly from this fresh flame

All at Once

for Jennie

All at once the ginkgo casts its golden crowns at our astonished feet. Fact is, the leaves were all green, not gold at all: the snow of the ginkgo, weirdly magical, having fallen all at once. *It's like the tree says it's done* my housemate emails me at work and *you won't believe the yard.* And I don't. I am certain a leaf blower has been involved, but no. I listen, rapt, as she describes the soft dripping sound as they fell all day while she was home. So I look it up and yes, this deciduous tree does this after first frost. *But how does it know?* I ask myself. A living fossil, the last of its species that is 270 million years old. One tree can live 3,000 years, its leaves medicinal for memory. Of course things can change all at once: suddenly a marriage is over, a loved one dead, a child grown and gone, a diagnosis received, but rarely does loss produce this show of beauty. All at once the ginkgo loosens its leaves in green snow and we are forced to smile in wonder.

SUN DOGS

Who, if I cried out, would hear me among the angels' hierarchies?
　　　　　　—Rilke, Duino Elegies

There is no hierarchy
All is circle
You can't get anywhere
from need, except to despair
Hypervigilance
serves me no more
Watching for danger
all the time
means I miss
the opportunity
for joy right here and now
The linear path is a lie

The dance was always
circular
This nimbus is too heavy
to bear, to wear, to bear to wear
You say sun dogs
mean severe cold
in their austere beauty
Our love halos us,
sets us apart
for service to one another
I remain suspicious of hope
and yet—sunflower

Missio Mei

I went all the way to Arizona
to try to forget you

That was my mission

But you are in every arroyo
We were always either flow or wash

Javelina scavenge the yard of my host
while rattlesnake guards front door

The Catalinas change
expressions every time I see them

My host remains expressionless

He insists we visit the Mission
White bones stark against blue sky

All water is holy,
but old habits die hard,

so I cross myself
with water from the font

of a religion that forced baptism
onto *heathens*,

forced innocence
from children

I see water turned to blood

Wooden painted saints
look on with sad indulgence

I could have lit a candle for a price
Instead I offer prayers in Cherokee

At the gift shop,
seeking some small kinship,

I buy an O'odham basket
woven from beargrass and yucca

Stepping back into the day
the sun tries to warm the chill between us

We do not walk up the hill,
even though that is what you want to do

I need no other vantage
I have seen enough

Hawk calls alarm as it crosses blue

When you smile your eyes stay flat
I remain expressionless

This is what happens
when you give away your power

Now my mission is to call it back

In Your Mind You Go to Water

There are still people who live on the land and do not objectify the Earth.
The pain of the earth is their pain.
    —Eduardo Duran

You were born with death within you

Passed on in blood,
trauma from prior generations, including the land
You try explaining this to the doctor:
the difference between pathology and blood memory

He takes furtive notes,
threatens dire consequences for noncompliance
His kind have been trained to try to train our brains
to eschew extremes of joy and pain,

have tried to stable unbroken horses of our dreams
while from the storehouse of memory
comes knowledge of sacrifice, Selu and Tsali,
and even now those willing to risk life

by raising one if manyed voice in defense of sacred land
But the white doctor writes on his white pad
prescriptions for Lethean lethargy
knowing docile people forget blood heritage,

docile people won't rise up
but rather acquiesce to colonizing "experts"
In the office of the oppressor
there is no room for voices and visions of elders

Rain dances outside window frame
In your mind you go to water, go to prayer
in solidarity with other suffering survivors
like your brave friend who said she'd take on the pain

of the People if only she could protect them
Goodbye, physician, who does harm first and last
We'll swallow no more pills, no more lies
Only pain prompts witness; anesthetization, apathy

You were born with strength within you

DRAW

Pull of seeking-self that underlies all outward artifice
You see blood everywhere
O positive

This is what happens when you give away your power
You have to call it back
Oh, positive

As blood draw draws and draws
you draw strength from remembering the way the body
of the mountain endures

Whatever happens to your body,
you know it will be returned to the land that holds
blood memories of ancestors, of loved ones, and this fills you with peace

Awi

I have made many mistakes,
but just this morning a deer shows me
the grace of release by being in the present

She steps out to greet me
and assesses my intent before
entering the orchard
to breakfast on the fallen apples

Unconcerned about her next steps,
she lets the sun warm her fur
as light diamond-patterns leaves

There is no rush
There is no self-recrimination
in her deerness
I watch to learn from her,

who has ceased watching me
I say to her *I have so many griefs*
She takes it in and breathes out peace

When she moves over the hill
and out of my sight,
I wish her blessing
as she has blessed me

I have made mistakes that I cannot undo
All I can do is what the deer taught me:
Be here now

In the Manner of Cottonwoods

Flagrant display, the way, that first night,
you pulled me to you with unexpected ardor

and the way we swayed, trunk to trunk, in slatted light
from parking lot and the way you said my eyes had gone to silver

Rise

When you finally
see people as they are
instead of how you wanted
to control them to be
you are forced to grieve
all you lost of yourself
in service to false premise,
false promise

You finally turn
compassion on yourself
and tend your own growth

For instance, this maple tree
outside my temporary window
is a life I envy
I've watched its limbs lashed by storm
denuded by winter wind and snow
and still come back full green in spring,
roots remaining firm
I vow to do the same

Trees communicate
and report knowledge
to each other, even warning
Trust yourself to know what to do
Trust what the ancestors are telling you even now
in this ceremony that is your life

Sursum Corda

Abnormality on EKG
when you were sick
with this new virus

And still your heart beats
even though you never think
to thank it

Black bear guarding cubs
Mother holding baby
as life-sustaining treatment
is withdrawn
Pietà in the PICU on the mo(u)rning
of Christ's Nativity

Gowned in PPE
you provide what comfort you can
You chart death with dry eyes
but cry on the way home
to rented room

Conveyance

Before the trauma before the fevers before the disappointments there
was a string of silver running through your life like this spider's line
cast from tree to windowpane, invisible except in certain light

These unseen trapezes transport us from past to present from now to
future, from life to death

What are you waiting for?
Did the wind not just etch your name into the slate of sky?

OREGON

Old betrayals float back to you
through the haze of fever
as this virus terrorizes
the territory of your body
That time in the high desert,
lunar landscape,
after your surgery
when you asked for a cup of hot tea,
but your husband refused,
so you had to move slowly, painfully
to get it for yourself
Gradually you realized
it was better to fulfill your own needs,
to make your own tea,
stirring in raw honey and cream
with sensuous swirls,
tasting freedom for the first time
and reading your future
in tea leaves that floated free

Psalm in Praise of Unknown Moons

Jupiter has sixty-seven moons that are known,
making the moon we know commonplace or rare,
depending on perspective
There are more moons than we'll ever see

That dark morning, on the way to the airport
the moon was a shallow saucer
and we wondered what it was called
I suggested *gibbous*, but turns out I was wrong

There is no name for the moon we saw
It was a trick of cloud, creating upturned crescent
Praise be both to known and named,
unknown and unnamed moons

THE QUIET EARTH

This healing isn't instantaneous
You have so much to let go of,
toxin on toxin
and you have lasting symptoms,
but seismologists say the world got quiet
when we all stayed home

The earth started to heal
when we stopped driving
Animals frolicked
in deserted streets
before they, too, succumbed
to sickness

When will we comprehend
that our fate is not
separate from the whole?

Goldfinch
delivers encomium
in honor of the sun
while carrion beetle
plumbs the mulch for flesh

QUILT

for Allison

The moments that leap and glitter above the water of memory:
the way your hair fell wet around you fresh from the shower, the
way I tucked you in at night, quilt over your feet, how you said it
was like the drape of a warm dog. I hold those memories close for
warmth when I recall dark drive to dawn airport then seeing you
off into the air, holding back tears on the ground

CZA

for Alex K.

You had just said *blessing*
in the course of conversation
when I happened to look up and see
the rainbow or a portion of one upside down
like a smile in the sky,
that later I will find is a kind of halo
called a circumzenithal arc

Once, while driving back from Winston,
I see a column of pink called a light pillar,
another kind of halo,
and recall the Bible verse about pillar of cloud and pillar of fire
and wonder at what guides us and who, if not Creator,
if not wisdom of elders who shine their light
on our own lives

We joke about heavenly signs
and yet we also hope
to find meaning there
Who's to say there's no significance?
Why not choose to allow ourselves awe
and rapturous humility
at what we marvel at but cannot understand?

FOLLOWING THE LIGHTS

The earth tilts
Sunlight recedes into snow

There has to be a balance
Dark is not evil

Light is not good
Those dualities serve only

to perpetuate the myth
born of need to control

Rather, seek out stories
for consolation and illumination

I receive an alert from an app
that tracks the aurora

The closest place to see it now
is a thousand miles away

You go
I'll follow

FEAST

Love bade me welcome…and I did eat
—*Herbert*

You are finally here at the banquet table:
you are loved
you are fed
you are held
you are safe

for now

ICING

You have high tolerance,
but it is difficult
All of us walking around
in pain of some kind
For instance, you tell me
your best friend was killed
long ago in Germany
You bore and bear this grief
even as you make me laugh
with your joy for life
We learn each other's sorrows
so we can help carry them together
and transform them into wisdom
for endurance
On your birthday you eat the cake,
I eat the icing
Our pain subsides
into sweetness
knowing today is the gift it always was

GOOD MEDICINE

for GIL

I.
For seven weeks
fever and chills
bind you to another world
Unknown birdsong your only companion
Dreams of the dead waiting to welcome you
Dreams about other parts of the house you thought were empty,
but were filled with the dead
Long ladle stirring the soup of your lungs
Struggling to breathe
Fluorescent lights in doctor's office look like bones
One lung goes quiet
Rabbit on patio stops and stares at you, a fellow creature,
through glass of sliding door
You envy his ability to move
Bits of blue in sky like river glass
Evening comes on like ether
You fear you may not survive this
You must get well for your son
though you are tired and ready to let go
You save a white spider from the sink on Easter Sunday
Dream you are dressed in gold sari at a party,
people laughing and smiling, the dead
waiting to welcome you in celebration,
but you're not ready yet
Dream you're gathering prayer books
No angels in attendance in this wilderness
Gift of birthday violets the office sends gives you purpose:
if you can keep them alive you will keep yourself alive
You name them and talk to them as weeks pass
The world outside your door and windows

has gone from the sickly green of early spring
with phlegmy yellow of forsythia
to full putrescence of summer
If you get through this,
you vow not to squander another day

II.
I remain too sick to move,
so a friend sends me medicine,
ginseng and tobacco,
prayers in our language
to make an offering
He says not to feed the illness,
not to give it power by naming it

Returning to tradition
is what began
my healing,
not all the Western medicine
that treated only symptoms,
not offending
imbalance

I turn to face the sun and offer prayers
to Creator in Cherokee
I am a new creation every morning
Thankful to be breathing,
I consecrate this illness
to a life of service,
grateful for even the smallest of blessings

CAN YOU, MY LOVE

You are more than the sum of what
has happened to you
Your scars tell the story
of outward hurts,
but what of the heart?
Its truculent beat
has persisted thus far
through the blood-remembered
loss of land and language,
through personal harms
You have lost a lot,
but others never had as much
The sickness of plague
is easy to read as
the outward and visible
sign of the sickness
of racism
rotting this country
founded on genocide
built on slavery
We can never get well
without the bravery
of protests,
without the vulnerability of shared story
without the healing power of ceremony
without the perseverance
of love in the face of hate
But these are all generalities
The question is,
can you, my love, arise
with unhardened heart
and give thanks for a day

of unknowns?
Can you heal what you
can within yourself
so that you become
a purer vessel
for the change we need to seek?

HELIANTHUS

On my way to you
I pass a field full of sun,
gold on gold,
and remember your saying
you are descended
from Mayans

Sun/sun dance

I grasp at happiness
as if for bright coin
from a well for wishing
You tell me instead to hope
and say to follow the sun
like these flowers in lambent light

BRINGING BACK THE FIRE

No one thought that I could do it (What good
could a water spider be?) I've never
known, I never knew, my own worth so could
not imagine being of use, not clever

like the rest. So I watched as those stronger
tried to retrieve the fire from the hollow
of a sycamore on the island where
Thunders sent lightning knowing we couldn't follow

because of the water that lay between.
Before that, the world was dark and cold
Fire promised warmth and life; without it, certain
death, not just for animals, but untold people

Council convened and sent each animal in turn
But one after another they failed
to bring back fire; instead they came back burned
and even today you can hear the tales

of how appearances were changed: wings
of raven ever blackened, owls with eyes
ringed white from smoke or changed to red by singe
of heat. Despite outward strength their enterprise

failed to bring back the fire. Even snakes tried
and returned scorched black, while darting through hot ash
made them move that way ever since. None died
but none succeeded in rash efforts

So I began to think just
maybe I could figure out
a way and be strong in mind
even if least expected
to contribute. They never
even noticed me. They stepped
past or over me as they

kept trying to bring back Fire
I waited until they were
all exhausted and marked out-
wardly and inwardly with
failure. I waited even
as they revived and began
to bluster about new plans

I waited as they all slept
in disbelief at their in-
ability to do what
was required to bring back fire
Meanwhile I began to pray:
Creator, we need this fire
or we will all die of cold

Everyone has failed thus far
If it is your will, use me
somehow to retrieve the fire
Just a small ember will do
I cannot compare to great
animals, who bear the marks
of ineffectual efforts

Help me figure out a way
to save not only Ani-
mals but also the People
Guide me, I prayed, *use me if*
I can be of any use
I honestly do not know
if this was said aloud

or not. So I prayed and did
not move from the water's bank
as others slept fitfully
around me or nursed their wounds
from their attempts, many now
unrecognizable from
gravely altered appearance

Finally everyone went
home, but tossed and turned in sleep,
uttering obscenities
in dreams of fire and water
And still I sat and waited
for an answer. I did not
eat. I did not mean to fast
but hours went by until I
no longer was alone: an-
cestors came and circled round

I thought maybe I had died,
but when I began to move
realized I was yet alive
Time was bending in different

ways: first I saw a blighted
world devoid of animals
or people, desolately
dark. Then I saw a brightening
glow that could only come from
fire I had managed to bring
back. But how? I was waiting

to be shown and then as if
in a dream I found myself
spinning a bowl with thread from
my own body. I knew (don't
ask me how) this was meant
to fit a bit of fire that
I would put on my back to

carry back and that was my
awaited answer that came
to me in solitude when
every sought-for thought had brought
forth naught

Since I am the kind of water spider
that can dive and also skim the surface
and have fur to keep me warm, I wasn't
afraid of the long swim to the island.
So after all this was shown to me I
told Council I would do it, I would be
the one who would go and bring back the fire.
But I do not think they even heard me,
since my voice was not loud and not a voice
they were used to hearing, not expecting
anything of note from one so small.

Determined, I took a deep breath, deep dive
then ventured towards the island through dark water.
Though by myself, I never felt alone.
I felt the strength of those who came before me,
so that when I finally got to the tree
where fire rested in hollow of the sycamore,
I carefully secured just a small coal,
an orange remnant and reverently placed
it in the bowl I'd made and affixed to my back.
It was only then that I knew I would
succeed in bringing back the sacred fire.

I didn't dive
on the way back,
so as not to douse the tender flame.
Instead I skated slowly on the surface to hold the basket steady.
Those looking from above would have seen only a small light
moving across the dark of water.
I barely made a ripple.
When I got back to shore
I half expected to see the faces of elders
and faces of children and people,
who, thanks to the fire, would now live and not die.

In my momentary hubris,
I imagined
they would have been too stunned to say anything.
I imagined
how they would have stood
around the small and emanating glow still snug in its bowl.

But they were all sleeping,
exhausted from their efforts,
so I quietly worked
to gather kindling
for a fire that would never die down again.

Once the fire was established,
I moved away to rest,
and from where I was outside the circle
I saw them begin to stir
in the warmth and light,
amazed at what had happened
while they were sleeping.

They began to speculate
about who had done it,
but I realized I did not need credit.
The important thing was it was done
and evidently they had not heard me volunteer,
which was just as well,
since I was tired
and wanted to retreat
and think about this thing that I had done,
but not alone.
It had come to me in inspiration
almost as if in a trance
and I knew I couldn't take the credit.
I knew the strength did not come from myself alone.
I was just the willing vessel.

I kept the bowl that I had made
to remind me
of what I could accomplish
out of strengths that I'd been given
I, too, was amazed at what had happened,
seemingly not from my volition

I dived deep, deeper than before,
air bubbles covering my body in silver beads like mercury

Down below the surface I retreated,
but looking up I could see the wavy movements
of those who stood on the shore
and looked across to the island,
wondering what had happened as they slept.
Their voices come as echoing sound,
but I folded some of my legs over my ears so as not to hear their words.

Later, when my story became known
(a child had heard me tell Council I had volunteered to go)
I heard it told and retold but it was not their narrative to tell.
For instance,
many think the bowl was empty going over,
but it wasn't.
It was filled with hope
and prayer
and humility born of necessity:
Use me for good
I said to myself over and over
as I traversed the water to the island,
praying Thunders were not watching.

No one ever thought that I could do it. Some still dispute it. But I carry my bowl still, my reminder to myself. Now that I am older and an elder, some of the younger water spiders come to me for lessons and eventually one of them will ask me to tell my story. It's hard to tell it without seeming that I think I am some kind of hero. But what they don't understand is that I knew that a greater Fire had filled me with enough light to see solution to a dire problem. I had made myself receptive to an unexpected answer. I think of this often as I rest beneath the water, how doubt is a dampening of spirit.

I brought back the fire. I never would have believed it.

Deep in the water
Deep in my bell of air
I dream dreams of fire and water
And when it thunders I think of the hollow in the sycamore tree on that island that once seemed impossible to reach

REMOVING THE HALO

Turns out having
the halo removed
hurts more than
getting it put on
As painful
as the tightening was,
the loosening
is worse
Reversal of pressure
causes more pain
as your head seems to expand,
but after the pain subsides
you feel lighter
You carry yourself taller,
with more awareness
You were
always your own
messenger,
carrying
your version of truth
You were always
enlightened,
but just didn't claim it,
instead looking outward
for someone else
to validate your worth
The halo was heavy and hurt,
but after adjusting to life without it,
there is lightness in the removal,
the beginning of healing
after apparatus of oppression
There is no end of pain in the world,

but there are healers
called to counteract the negative force,
those who offer sacrifice in service of others,
those who help make meaning
from the wreckage,
since the weight
of their halo demands it
You weren't allowed to save
the halo's pins, but you saved
the staples that zagged
like a zipper down the side
of your scalp
You palmed them lightly
their dull silver
flecked with reddened rust
of dried blood,
fetish proof
of survival
As a child
you had a nimbus
of light hair
Now it barely
grows
back white
after radiation's
obliteration
You remember how
you waited for someone
to come hold your hand
and calm your fear
That never happened
Instead, you learned
not to need
a hand to hold

You can hold your own
You can hold this scalpel
of a pen, excising what is still
dis-eased
Blunt as this instrument may be
you can still write your own
hagiography,
exposing yourself as
flawed
like everyone else
All of us doing our best
with our augmented
halos of self-aggrandizement
and in that
exposure,
seeing with compassionate truth,
with the grace of self-reckoning
Remembrance
of the heaviness
of halo
contrasted with the lightness
of removal
The acceptance
of aloneness
that frees you
for transcendence

Notes:

"Apparatus": "The Bakken formation of western North Dakota contains one of the largest oil deposits in the country. New technology has made it feasible to extract these resources. Most oil is extracted by hydraulic fracturing - commonly known as 'fracking.' This technique fractures the bedrock, using a slurry of sand, chemicals, and water to extract the trapped oil. Environmental impacts from spilled oil and fracking fluids are omnipresent with the fossil fuel industry. Many wells tap into natural gas reserves, but lack the infrastructure to collect and store this less-valuable fuel source. The gas is wasted as it is burned off by on-site flaring. The extraction and use of fossil fuels releases greenhouse gases, altering the global carbon cycle. As society struggles to cope with a changing climate, we must question our use of these critical resources—now more than ever."
https://www.nps.gov/thro/learn/nature/bakken-oil.htm

"Affixing the Halo": "Uneasy is the head that wears a halo" is an obvious play on Shakespeare's "uneasy is the head that wears a crown," often phrased as "heavy is the head that wears the crown."

"Square of Blue": Maslow's hierarchy of needs is a theory of motivation that states that five categories of human needs dictate an individual's behavior: physiological needs, safety needs, love and belonging needs, esteem needs, and self-actualization needs. Thank you to Robert F. Fox for sharing that Indigenous (Blackfoot) wisdom may have inspired Maslow's theory:
https://www.resilience.org/stories/2021-06-18/the-blackfoot-wisdom-that-inspired-maslows-hierarchy/

"Missio Mei": The title is a subversion of Missio Dei, the Church's mission to impose Christianity on "heathens" of Indigenous populations, a form of cultural genocide.

"Red Clay": Red Clay (Tennessee) was the site of the last seat of the Cherokee government before the 1838 enforcement of the Indian Removal Act of 1830, which resulted in The Trail of Tears. Before the site was a government council site, it was used for many different Cherokee rituals due to its famous spring named the Blue Hole Spring. The site is considered sacred.

"Media Vita": "in the midst of life" (we are in death/in morte sumus). From the Burial of the Dead in the Book of Common Prayer.

"How to Make it Through to the End of a Conjure": after Joy Harjo's, "Songs from the House of Death, or How to Make it Through to the End of a Relationship."

"Trauma Box": name for area in the trauma bay, where there are assigned places for each person's role, a careful choreography designed to minimize confusion and maximize efficiency in a small space where it can be a matter of life and death.

"Sursum corda": "Lift up your hearts;" from the Latin Mass.

"Awi": the title is the Cherokee word for "deer."

"Psalm in Praise of Unknown Moons": psalms of Hebrew poetry in biblical tradition are often in praise or lament.

"CZA": Exodus 13: 21-22 "The Lord went in front of them in a pillar of cloud by day, to lead them along the way, and in a pillar of fire by night, to give them light, so that they might travel by day and by night. Neither the pillar of cloud by day nor the pillar of fire by night left its place in front of the people."

"Bringing Back the Fire": based on traditional Cherokee story of how the water spider brought fire to the People in a basket on her back.

Acknowledgments

Thank you once again to Weymouth Center for residencies that enabled me both to start and finish this book. Special thanks to Alex Klalo, Director of Property Management, for hospitality and help over my many years coming "home" to Weymouth

Thank you to the following journals where some of these poems appeared, sometimes in different form:

Claw & Blossom: "Call"

North Dakota Quarterly: "Bringing Back the Fire," "In Your Mind You Go to Water," "Missio Mei"

Axon (Australia): "In the Manner of Cottonwoods" and "Ventus"

Westerly (Australia): "Heimweh"

Red Flag Poetry: "Red Clay"

With thanks for all I learned from Mary Burks, supervisor, and from colleagues during residency. Thank you to all my patients whom I was honored to serve

With appreciation to Allison Hedge Coke, who knew this would be my next book before I did

Thank you to the wonderful Spuyten Duyvil team for welcoming a second book of mine

With gratitude to Robert F. Fox for introducing me to the beauty of North Dakota

Of mixed descent, including Cherokee, KIMBERLY L. BECKER is author of four other poetry collections: *Words Facing East* and *The Dividings* (WordTech Editions), *The Bed Book* (Spuyten Duyvil), and *Flight* (MadHat Press). Her poems appear widely in journals and anthologies, including *Indigenous Message on Water*; *Women Write Resistance: Poets Resist Gender Violence*; and *Tending the Fire: Native Voices and Portraits*. Her work has been nominated for a Pushcart. She has received grants from Maryland, New Jersey, and North Carolina, and has been awarded residencies at Hambidge, Weymouth, and Wildacres. Kimberly has read at Busboys and Poets, The National Museum of the American Indian (Washington, DC), Split This Rock, and Wordfest. She has served as mentor for PEN America's Prison Writing and AWP's Writer to Writer programs. She currently lives in North Dakota, but calls the mountains of North Carolina home.   kimberlylbecker.com